# A NEW SENSE OF PURPOSE

With unusual fervor and spiritual outpouring, the huge crowd lifted its voice in the opening hymn. With one mighty voice came the words "Onward Christian Soldiers." Then Dr. King rose to speak and the crowd was silent. The television cameras began to roll—the Montgomery bus boycott had become *news*.

"Love must be our regulating ideal," Dr. King stressed in his clear, strong voice. . . .

"If you will protest courageously, and yet with dignity and Christian love, when the history books are written in future generations, the historians will have to pause and say, 'There lived a great people—a black people—who injected new meaning and dignity into the veins of civilization.' This is our challenge and our overwhelming responsibility."

# MARTIN LUTHER KING:

## The Peaceful Warrior

# MARTIN LUTHER KING:
# The Peaceful Warrior

### ED CLAYTON
Illustrated by David Hodges

**AN ARCHWAY PAPERBACK**
Published by POCKET BOOKS • NEW YORK

FRONT COVER NOTE: The photograph shows Dr. King and his wife, Coretta Scott King.

Final chapter *Free at Last* written by Hermona Clayton

An Archway Paperback published by
POCKET BOOKS, a division of Simon & Schuster, Inc.
1230 Avenue of the Americas, New York, N.Y. 10020

ISBN: 0-671-63119-5

First Pocket Books printing September, 1969

22  21  20  19  18  17  16  15  14  13

AN ARCHWAY PAPERBACK and colophon are
registered trademarks of Simon & Schuster, Inc.

Printed in the U.S.A.

IL 4+

# Contents

# The Hard Way Up

"Someday," whispered Martin Luther King, Jr., to his mother as they sat together in church listening to a guest speaker, "I'm going to have *me* some big words like that."

Mrs. Alberta King looked at her eleven-year-old son with quiet gentleness and pride. "I'm sure you will, son," she whispered back. And to herself she thought, "It will be a lot easier for him to come by his *big* words than it was for his father before him."

She knew that if young Martin were

called to the work, he would very likely follow his father as pastor of Ebenezer Baptist Church. But, her husband, Martin, Sr., had not had a ready-made berth to step into. He had *fought* for his place in the world, with sweat and raw determination.

Mrs. King mused on, only half hearing the rich voices of the choir. Her father, the Reverend Adam Daniel Williams, had served as the pastor of Ebenezer Baptist Church for thirty-seven years. He had practically built it up from the ground. Martin, Sr., had taken over as pastor when his father-in-law had died, but he had taken many giant steps first. Martin, Sr., was a sharecropper's son. He was born on a rundown farm in Stockbridge, Georgia, at the turn of the century— December 19, 1899. Long before he had even seen the inside of a schoolhouse, he was at work in the fields with his ten brothers and sisters, helping to plant and harvest their meager crops of cotton and corn. Until Martin, Sr., was fifteen, he never had more than three months of schooling in any one year.

Even on school days Martin, Sr., had his chores. He was up at dawn to *curry*, or brush down, the family's two mules. His schoolmates often teased him because they said he even smelled like a mule!

"I may *smell* like a mule," he once snapped back, "but I don't *think* like one!"

Martin, Sr.'s, best subject was always arithmetic. Somehow it made the most sense to him and had more to do with his daily life than any of his other subjects. He often gave himself examples to work out that were not to be found in his textbooks.

He would set himself problems like this to figure out: "Most of us, except Mama, work in the fields all day, every day, but Sunday. That's usually twelve of us. Now, if you took all those hours and multiplied them by the twelve of us it would

3

turn out a *lot* of hours. The boss," he continued to himself, referring to the white man who owned their farm, "don't work half that time—yet he gets *half* of what twelve of us earns. That just don't make sense as arithmetic," he muttered to himself.

Martin's arithmetic stood the King family in good stead at harvest time one year. The boss was "doing the figuring" on the Kings' crop. Martin's father, James Albert King, was standing passively by. Mr. King could barely read and write and he was very respectful of the boss' knowledge of figures. When the boss had finished he turned to Martin's father with a grin. "Well, we're all even," he said.

What the boss meant by "even" was that Mr. King's *share* of his cotton crop would be just enough to pay for the food and other supplies that the Kings had bought for credit at the boss' store during the past winter. Being *even* also meant that Mr. King would receive no cash for the long months of labor that he and his family had put into the crop. And there would be no hope of his receiving any cash for a whole year, until the next harvest. But, Mr. King knew that, as surely as night follows day, he would be in debt again at the boss' store when they settled up *next* year. It seemed that no matter how hard all of them worked they never got *ahead*.

But this year it was to be different. Young Martin had been quietly observing the boss' figuring with an eagle eye. He did not quite have the courage to address a white man directly, but he said to his father, "Papa, the boss *forgot* to add in over seven and a half sacks of seed—and that amounts to almost a thousand dollars."

Even *half* a thousand dollars seemed like a fortune to the Kings. Martin smiled to himself. With all that money he could see the whole family going to church

5

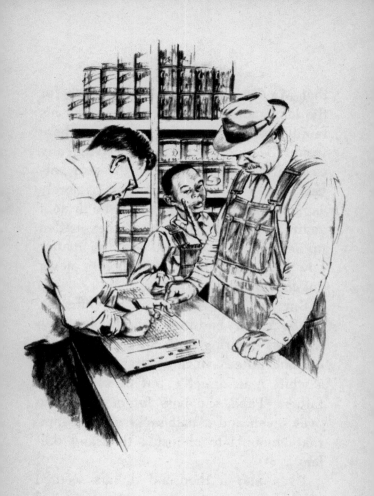

"Papa, the boss forgot to add in our seven and a half sacks
of seed—and that amounts to almost a thousand dollars."

dressed in the finest. And wouldn't Mama be proud and pleased?

But the boss was not pleased. The boss had not *forgotten* the seed—he had merely conveniently overlooked it. "Just you remember," he threatened Martin, "I don't stand for no troublemakers. If you get uppity and forget your place, I'm going to run you off my land. Y'hear?"

Martin heard but he wasn't satisfied with what he heard. He was still working on his own kind of arithmetic. "How come," he wondered, "we work all those hours and we live in a rundown, leaky old shack, and the boss works less and he lives in a big fine house? Why is it that *we* always wind up with just about nothing?"

When Martin was fifteen he left the farm for good and went to Atlanta, twenty miles away, to find work. He could no longer stand the dragging, sad round of defeat and despair. He did not think that a week of back-breaking work for a few hours of forgetfulness in strong drink was a good way of life. It was his father's way. But it was not Martin's.

Martin was sure that more schooling would help him make a better life for himself, and that's what he set out to get. Of course, he had to work during the day to support himself, and the only jobs open to Negroes in those days were the hard jobs.

He hauled freight in a railroad yard and learned to stoke an engine. He was still a growing boy and he pushed his strength to the utmost and beyond, every working day. The meals that he could afford didn't give him much to grow on, either.

At night he got cleaned up and put on his one neat, dark suit and went to school. Sometimes he could hardly stay awake in class. Many times he was so discouraged that he was almost ready to quit—but he didn't.

It took Martin Luther King, Sr., eleven long years to work his way through high school and he was twenty-six years old when he got his diploma.

Five years later, when he graduated from Morehouse College, he was already a minister, a husband and a father, having married Alberta Williams when he was still in school. Their first child, Willie Christine ("Chris"), was born in Grandfather Williams' spacious twelve-room house on Auburn Avenue in Atlanta, Georgia.

The Reverend King had come a long way from the rundown farm on which he was born.

# The Ghetto
# and the Church

Martin Luther King, Jr., was the middle child in his family. He was born on January 15, 1929, a year after his sister, Chris, and a year before his brother, "A. D.," who had been christened Alfred Daniel.

All of the King children were born in their grandfather Williams' house. In those days, there was not even the hope that a Negro might choose the neighborhood where he wanted to live. In cities and towns all over the United States, Negroes could only live in the *colored section,* and this was much like living in a *ghetto*—those walled cities within cities into which the Jews were herded in Europe.

Most of the Kings' neighbors on Auburn Avenue and the few adjacent streets that made up the Atlanta ghetto, had only one thing in common—they were all Negroes. Some of them were uneducated field hands. When they came to Atlanta they got the menial jobs only—as janitors or garbage men. Some of them could not find steady work. Those who had never been taught a trade worked as day laborers when there were buildings to be built or ditches to be dug. When there was no work to be done, their families went hungry.

Some of the women were luckier than the men. They had been trained as house servants. They could always find jobs as cooks and maids in Atlanta's many prosperous white homes. Often the mother of a Negro family was able to earn more as a servant than her husband could earn as an unskilled laborer. These homes were restless and unhappy. Men like to provide for their families—not leave it up to their womenfolk.

But there were a few who prospered in the ghetto, too. There was a handful of college graduates. Most of them had entered the professions, being among the first Negro teachers, lawyers, doctors and dentists. Like Martin's father, they had been strong enough to work their way up against terrible odds and everyone in the neighborhood was proud of them.

There were even some Negro-owned businesses on Auburn Avenue—a bank, two insurance companies and a drugstore that grew into a chain of five drugstores throughout the city. In fact, there was a Negro who was *almost* a millionaire on Auburn Avenue.

The heart of the Atlanta ghetto was

centered in its churches. There were three of them within six blocks on Auburn Avenue. Ebenezer Baptist Church was Martin's family's church. His grandfather served as pastor there for thirty-seven years. Martin was two when his grandfather died, at sixty-eight, preparing his Sunday sermon. But the church remained in the family, with Martin's father taking over as pastor.

All the time that Martin was growing up, the church was his second home. Through it, he felt the heartbeat of his neighborhood. He heard his father preach a new way of life to his neighbors. The fiery young pastor begged his people to hold their heads high and not to take abuse from anyone, but always "to walk humbly with your God." When their steps faltered and they were in need, Martin watched his mother and his grandmother pack baskets of food for them.

He grew up with the Bible and the

words of Christ as living things. He knew early what it meant to his neighbors to "turn the other cheek," and what it cost them to love their enemies or to "do unto others as you would have others do unto you."

By the time Martin was four, his clear, young voice was heard singing solos on Sunday mornings at Ebenezer. Soon other Negro congregations wanted to hear him, too, and his mother often took him to smaller churches in nearby towns to sing.

The tiny boy with his true, rich voice moved his hearers deeply. In the small towns where people had not yet learned quiet "city ways," the end of one of Martin's hymns was always greeted with fervent "Amens" and "Praise the Lord." Many a small church almost rocked with joy after Martin sang. People clapped and "got the spirit" and sometimes Martin felt almost frightened by the noise. Services were much quieter at Ebenezer.

By the time Martin was four, his clear, young voice was heard singing solos on Sunday mornings at Ebenezer.

The people in the small-town churches showed their appreciation of Martin in another way, too. Often when he sang, the "thank-offering," or collection, was a big one. And young as Martin was, he knew this was a good thing. Maybe some of the money would be added to the fund for a new church roof, or perhaps there would be children wearing new clothes when they started school—children who might have gone in rags if Martin had not sung.

# Schooldays

When Martin's big sister, Chris, turned six and started school, five-year-old Martin *insisted* that he was grown-up enough to go, too. He was so passionate in his pleas that he finally convinced his mother to take him along.

Martin's mother was a schoolteacher and she recognized that her son was an exceptionally bright child, so she decided to enroll him in the first grade, hoping that he could pass as a six-year-old.

But Martin didn't remain in school long. Soon after he started, he let the secret of his real age slip out. He was telling the other children in his class about his most recent birthday party.

"And there were *five* candles on my cake," he said proudly. His teacher overheard him and that was the end of Martin's schooling until the following year. But he hadn't been in school long before he was skipped into his sister Chris' grade, after all!

Soon after Martin started school he began to spell out the signs in his neighborhood and around the city. One of the first things he learned to read was "For White Only." He seldom rode in streetcars or buses because his mother or father usually drove him in the family car, but when he did, there were still more signs to read. There was, "Colored seat from the rear" and "Colored exit by rear door." Little by little, he was becoming more aware of what it meant to be a Negro living in the deep South.

It was around this time that Martin

began to notice a few rather special things about his father, the Reverend King.

One day as he and his father were driving downtown, they were stopped by a policeman. "Let's see your license, *boy*," the cop drawled to Martin's father. Like most Southerners, the policeman addressed *all* Negro men, even venerable *old* men, with the belittling "boy." The Reverend King reached for his license, but before he handed it to the policeman he said, pointing to Martin, "He's a *boy*— I'm a *man!*"

Another time, his father took Martin downtown to buy him a pair of shoes. The white clerk came bustling over. He was courteous, but firm. "I'd be glad to serve you, if you'd sit in those seats at the back of the store," he said.

"Nothing wrong with these seats, thank you," Reverend King answered pleasantly. The clerk was embarrassed, but firmer. "But we don't serve *colored* in the front of the store," he tried to explain. "If you don't serve colored in the front of the store, you don't serve *these* colored at all," said the Reverend King, and he took Martin by the hand and marched out.

Of course, things like this didn't come up every day in the week; sometimes months would go by without an incident. Martin spent a lot of time climbing the big oak tree in the yard next door, or sitting in its shade and reading. Sometimes he would fly a kite with his brother, A.D., or skate on the sidewalk in front of his house with Chris.

Every so often there was a softball game in the vacant lot next door. One day, when they were playing baseball, Martin and A.D. were on opposite teams. Martin was catching for his team.

When it was A.D.'s turn at bat, he missed the ball but the bat flew out of his hand and smashed into Martin, who was squatting at home plate. There was a sickening thud and Martin was knocked

"Nothing wrong with these seats, thank you,"
Reverend King answered pleasantly.

flat. He lay on the ground, pale and still.

"You OK?" A.D. kept asking his brother. After what seemed a long, long time, Martin sat up. "Sure, I'm OK," he said to his brother, "but you're not—that was your third strike—and you're OUT!"

One of Martin's roughest childhood experiences occurred when he was six. A white shopkeeper on Auburn Avenue told her two sons they could no longer play with Martin "because he's colored." The three boys had been firm friends, and Martin did not forget this.

Five years later, he still bore a deep scar from the incident. And one day, while shopping downtown with his mother, Martin had another bad experience. Usually, Martin liked to go shopping. He liked the hustle and bustle, and he especially liked seeing the toys and fine clothes in the downtown stores.

Suddenly, a white woman popped out

of the crowd of shoppers. She planted herself directly in front of Martin and said the hate-filled word that Martin had always dreaded. "You're the little *nigger* who stepped on my foot," she bellowed. And before Martin could answer her, she lifted her hand and slapped his face— hard. Then she disappeared into the crowd again.

Like so many of his people before him, Martin was being taught about *prejudice* the hard way. He had looked the word up in his dictionary and found that it came from two Latin words—*prae*, before, and *judicium*, judgment. The definition said that prejudice was "an opinion formed without just grounds."

"The white lady," Martin told his mother, "certainly formed her opinion of me *without just grounds!*"

# Think
# Before You Act

Martin was small for his age and the big bullies looked upon him as a safe target. He soon found out that fighting back would get him nowhere. Still, he was not a coward and refused to run when he was challenged. So he learned to stand up for his rights by *talking* his way out of trouble.

Even A.D., who was a year younger, was a shade taller and more robust than his "big brother," and this rankled Martin. One day, A.D. was teasing Chris. She begged him to stop and so did Martin. But A.D. kept right on teasing her.

Finally Chris burst into tears. Without thinking, Martin picked up the telephone receiver and clouted A.D. on the head. A.D. went out like a light and did not come to until several anxious moments had passed. A.D. developed an egg-sized bump on his head of which he was very proud. But Martin did not like himself for days afterwards because he had struck his brother.

Fairly often Martin seemed compelled to do things without thinking. Usually they were the kind of things that got him into trouble and made him feel guilty.

Martin and A.D. shared a bike and Martin used to make his brother angry by taking very long turns with it. Sometimes he would disappear for a whole afternoon and A.D. didn't think this was fair.

The boys had been forbidden to ride anywhere but on the sidewalk and they had been cautioned to stay in their own neighborhood. But Martin just *had* to see what other neighborhoods looked like.

One spring day, Martin took a friend for a ride on the handlebars of his bike. They headed downtown to see what they could see. When they got into the crowded downtown section Martin had a hard time dodging in and out among the pedestrians. He edged his bike off the sidewalk and into the traffic. Before he had gone a block he was sideswiped by a truck. He and his rider were thrown from the bike and the next thing Martin knew a neighbor was bending over him.

The boys and the mangled bike were brought home by the neighbor, who had been driving by when the accident occurred.

Both boys were badly shaken up and black and blue all over. But, worst of all, Martin had to face A.D., who was pretty cross about the condition of *their* bike. "I've got to think things out better before

I go ahead and do them," Martin told himself.

Actually, Martin was always upset when he did anything that hurt anyone, particularly a member of his family. He was especially devoted to his mother, whom he always called "Mother-dear," and to his grandmother, Mrs. Jennie Williams, whom he called "Mama."

Often on Saturday nights, Martin's mother stayed up late to cook the family's Sunday dinner so that she could go to church with them the next day. Martin liked to stay up to help her. He would fire the furnace, or carry out the garbage, or maybe peel potatoes. Sometimes he would just sit and talk to his mother, to keep her company while she worked.

His grandmother was a pleasant-faced, cheerful woman and Martin always enjoyed being around people who were pleasant and had kind words to say. When Martin's mother or father spanked him for disobedience, Mama's kind words would help to heal his hurt. Martin was Mrs. Williams' favorite grandchild and she made no attempt to hide it. The two of them were very close.

One Sunday, when Martin was twelve, the family had gone to church together as usual. After the service, Mrs. Williams had left them to go to another church where she was to be the guest speaker at a woman's day program.

The rest of the family went home to dinner—except Martin. He sneaked off and headed downtown to see a parade, an activity which was strictly forbidden on the Lord's Day.

As Martin stood watching the parade he saw a friend push his way through the crowd to reach him. The boy had been sent by the family. In a breathless rush of words he told Martin that his grandmother was dead.

Mrs. Williams had suffered a heart attack at the church where she was to speak. She had been rushed to the hospital but had died before reaching it.

Martin felt that the judgment of God had been visited upon him because he had gone to a forbidden parade. He felt *responsible* for his grandmother's death.

When he got home the family had already gathered to mourn and the house was filled with neighbors and church members who had come to console them.

Martin's eyes darted from one face to another. Reddened eyes stared back at him—accusingly, he thought. He looked for his mother in whose face he hoped to find forgiveness. Finally his eyes met hers. Without saying a word, she buried her face in her handkerchief and wept.

Martin did not know what to do. *If only he hadn't gone to the parade!* He stumbled up the stairs. He knew only that he wanted to escape the accusing eyes. He had no plan when he threw open the rear window on the second floor. For

—and then he jumped!

a moment, he looked down at the peaceful, green quiet of the garden—and then
he jumped!

When Martin picked himself up a few
minutes later, he discovered that his
bruises were minor. "Praise the Lord," he
whispered.

The phrase reminded him of something
way back in his experience. Yes, he had
it! The small churches where he sang as a
boy. He remembered the swelling "Praise
the Lord" and the "Amens" and the
shouting that had frightened him. It was
the lack of control that had made him
afraid then, and it was his own lack of
control that he was facing now.

For a long while Martin sat on the
grass, nursing his bruises and thinking
very hard.

During the sad hours of his grandmother's burial, Martin contained his
grief with quiet control. People said that
he had grown up overnight.

# The Dream Begins

The Reverend King never wanted his boys to be *soft* even though he was able to make their childhoods a lot easier than his had been. He always insisted that if they wanted spending money they had better work for it! And what was more, they had better do a good job, or answer to him.

Martin began selling Atlanta's evening newspaper, *The Atlanta Journal,* as soon as he was big enough to lift the huge bundles of newspapers and to get a route of his own. He proved so responsible that

by the time he was thirteen he had been
promoted to assistant manager of one of
the newspaper's neighborhood deposit
stations.

One of the things Martin liked best to
do with the money he earned was buy
books—special books. He had long since
found out that the history books he was
given in school had very little in them
about *Negro* history and he was determined to find out more about his own
people.

After Martin finished the sixth grade,
his parents sent him to a private "laboratory" school which was being conducted
as an experiment by Atlanta University.
The classes were small and the students
were given a great deal of individual at-
tention by expert teachers who were ea-
ger to prove that Negro children could
learn just as quickly as white children if
they were given *an equal opportunity*.

Unfortunately, this fine school closed
down two years after Martin entered. But

he learned many things there that he had not even dreamed of as a public school student.

He learned of the giants and the heroes among his own people—those who had fought for Negro freedom and whose names were seldom mentioned in American history books.

He read of Harriet Tubman, the frail Negro slave who plotted and masterminded escape routes to the North for other runaway slaves; and of Nat Turner and Denmark Vesey, who led the slaves into uprisings and rebellions against their cruel plantation masters. His imagination reeled when he read of Frederick Douglass and his lifelong fight to abolish slavery—Frederick Douglass who was born a slave and became a statesman.

He thought often of the fact that no effective laws had been passed to help the Negro since Abraham Lincoln issued the Emancipation Proclamation in 1863. Although the Supreme Court had handed down one decision that it was not legal for white children and Negro children to be separated, or *segregated*, in the schools—he knew that there was still segregation in most of the schools in the South.

He knew that he would be proud to be like those heroes when he was a man. In his imagination, he could see himself as Nat Turner or as Denmark Vesey, leading his brothers to freedom in the dead of night. Or he would dream that he stood on a platform and, like Frederick Douglass, made fiery speeches about a better life for Negroes.

The time had come for Martin to "get the big words" that he had once told his mother he would find someday. And get them he did. Martin learned to use his big words very well.

By the time Martin was a junior in high school, he was using his big words so well that he was chosen, along with several other students, to represent his

Or, he would dream that he stood on a platform and, like Frederick Douglass, made fiery speeches about a better life for Negroes.

school in an oratorical contest in Valdosta, Georgia. Making the trip with them was their speech teacher, Miss Sarah Grace Bradley.

Martin did not win the contest, but he took second prize for his school.

On the way home, when the group boarded the bus for Atlanta, the students sat in whatever seats were vacant. A short distance up the road, however, more passengers got on the bus. Most of them were white.

When the white passengers could not find seats, the bus driver turned around and ordered the Negroes, old and young alike, to stand so that the white passengers could sit down. Several of the older Negroes began to get up, but Martin and the other students remained in their seats and ignored the driver.

This made the driver angry. He began shouting hate-words at them. Still they didn't move. Then he threatened to call the police. The students kept sitting. Finally their teacher asked them to stand. At first, none of them moved. Then slowly, one by one, they stood. And they had to remain standing for most of the ninety miles back to Atlanta.

Miss Bradley feebly tried to explain to the students that she felt it was her duty to avoid trouble since she was responsible for them. They listened, but they were not convinced.

Yet, Martin wondered, what else could she have done?

# The Choice

At fifteen, Martin was ready to enter college—for he had made such giant strides at the laboratory school that he was able to skip the ninth and the eleventh grades.

When Martin entered Morehouse College in Atlanta as a freshman in 1944, this great Negro institution was already sixty-five years old. Its founder was a Negro minister, the Reverend William Jefferson White, and it was supported by both Negro and white Baptists. Its students were all Negro.

Morehouse was respected as a school that produced great men. Among its graduates were many presidents of Negro colleges and scores of doctors, lawyers and teachers. Morehouse had graduated countless ministers, too—among them Martin's own father.

Everyone felt certain that Martin would follow his father into the ministry. The Reverend King took it for granted. But Martin was not sure. Above everything else, he wanted to choose a career in which he could help his people in the best way possible.

His mother sensed his indecision and suggested that Martin become a doctor. Maybe his mother was right, Martin thought. Perhaps he should become a doctor as she wished. As a doctor, he would be able to help his people to lower the high rate of disease among them.

Or, what about being a lawyer, he wondered. As a lawyer he would have the opportunity to use his speaking skills to help his people have *their* day in court.

It was always like this. Whenever he tried to make up his mind about a career, the thought came to Martin that he could not commit himself until he found *the work* that would make it possible for him to do his people the most good.

Even though Martin had not yet decided on a career, he chose Sociology and English as his majors. Sociology would give him an understanding of the behavior of people, and English would help him become a better speaker—a good start toward *something*, he was sure.

In the end, it was an essay that helped Martin make up his mind—Henry David Thoreau's "Civil Disobedience."

Eighty years before in Concord, Massachusetts, Thoreau had refused to cooperate with unjust laws. He had even *gone to jail* for what he thought was right. Thoreau felt that the poll tax law which required him to *pay* for the right to vote was unjust. So he did not pay his poll tax for six years but insisted upon his right to vote anyway. Then he was arrested and jailed.

Martin read and re-read Thoreau's essay, and little by little he began to see that Thoreau's technique of *civil disobedience* might be used to help the Negroes gain their rights. Why not simply refuse to obey laws that upheld the abuse and mistreatment of Negroes?

At last, Martin had struck upon something that *might* help the Negro on the road toward freedom.

As thought of civil disobedience took root in Martin's mind, he began to realize that he would have to try to get his ideas across to *many* Negroes if they were to succeed. Couldn't he best come before his people as a man of God, a minister, he wondered. A *new* kind of minister who would lead his people to freedom!

The more Martin thought about it, the

more the idea of becoming a minister felt right to him. But he kept his decision to himself and prayed for guidance. He wanted to be absolutely sure that he had a vocation.

By this time, Martin was nearing the end of his junior year in college and he still had to help pay for his senior year. That summer he joined A.D. and several of their friends and went to Simsbury, Connecticut, to work in the tobacco fields.

Martin knew that if a student was careful with what he earned, he could return home with as much as three or four hundred dollars to help toward his tuition. Working in Connecticut also gave Martin the chance to enjoy Northern freedom. On weekends, he and A.D. went to town with their friends. They were free to go to *any* motion picture theater, or to eat in *any* restaurant that they could afford.

The work, of course, was hard—picking and stripping the tobacco leaves on the

That summer he joined A. D. and several of their friends and went to Simsbury, Connecticut, to work in the tobacco fields.

seemingly endless stretches of farmland, day in and day out in the oppressive heat of a blistering sun.

When Martin returned to Atlanta, his mind was made up. He let it be known that he had been "called" to preach. Shortly after he entered the senior class at Morehouse, eighteen-year-old Martin was ordained as a minister and elected assistant pastor of Ebenezer Baptist Church.

It was a jubilant day for everyone—particularly Martin's father.

# Getting Ready

Now it was clear to Martin where he wanted to go. His interest in religion was beginning to take on new meaning. His passion for philosophy, fired by the writings of Thoreau, led him into a constant and exciting search for other writers and philosophers. These, he believed, would supply him with the additional knowledge that he needed to fight injustice.

In June, 1948, Martin was graduated from Morehouse College, but he did not yet feel that he had enough education to be the kind of minister that he wanted to be. So, he took advantage of the scholarship he had been awarded and decided to enter Crozer Theological Seminary in Chester, Pennsylvania.

Now Martin would *really* be on his own. This would not be like going to college at Morehouse where he had divided his time between school and home. At Crozer, he would be living six hundred miles away from home in the North— and competing with white students.

He began feeling a new sense of adulthood and personal responsibility. He would be one of six Negroes in a student body of about a hundred whites. He knew that in a sense he would always be on exhibit and he was determined that no action of his would ever let his people down.

Making friends always had been easy for Martin and Crozer was a friendly place. But there was one student from North Carolina who seemed unwilling to accept Negroes as his fellow students. In referring to Negroes, he often used the word *darkie*, another insulting name which Negroes do not like.

Martin did not become fully aware of how the student from North Carolina felt toward Negroes until he became involved in an incident with him. It grew out of a prank. Whenever a group of them found another student out of his room, they would go in and tear the room up by its roots. They upended his desk and chairs and made such a shambles of the room that it would take several hours to clean up the mess.

The student from North Carolina had joined in the fun several times but one day he returned to find that his own room had received the treatment. Immediately he went to Martin and accused him of doing the job out of spite. Then he pulled out a gun and threatened to shoot Martin.

Calmly, Martin denied that he had even been in the group that had over-

Then he pulled out a gun and threatened to shoot Martin.

turned the room. By now, fellow students began gathering around the two and the student from North Carolina was persuaded to put up his gun.

But the matter did not end there. It was brought before both the student government board and the faculty. Martin refused to press charges. Finally the white student admitted that he had been in the wrong and publicly apologized. In later years he and Martin became very good friends.

At Crozer, much of Martin's study was devoted to the teachings of Jesus and to the writings of other great leaders of all faiths. He became acquainted with the life and teachings of the great and gentle Indian leader, Mohandas K. Gandhi, the *Mahatma*, who had been able to free his people from British oppression with *nonviolent* methods.

Like Thoreau, Gandhi rebelled at laws which he considered unjust. But Gandhi went further than Thoreau. He taught his followers to *break laws* which seemed harsh and unjust, to allow themselves to be arrested and to accept the clubbings of the police without running away or striking back. He taught *love* for the oppressor—not hate.

Here, at last, Martin realized, was the long-awaited *method* to deal with the unjust laws that kept the Negroes only half-free.

Why not combine the teachings and ideas of Jesus Christ, Thoreau and Mahatma Gandhi, Martin asked himself. Had Jesus not said, "Love your enemies?" Did not Thoreau and Gandhi rebel against unjust laws? And had not Gandhi already shown that love had helped to end persecution for an entire nation?

Martin's mind reeled with the possibilities of such a method. It could work. He *knew* it could.

But how to get it across? Where? When?

It would not be easy to bring this new idea to Negroes.

He would just have to be patient and wait for the right moment.

# The Dream Unfolds

The three years at Crozer slipped past quickly. Living in the North most of each year gave Martin a chance to know white people who were on his side. But Martin also discovered prejudice in the North. There were no "For White Only" signs but some places still did not welcome Negroes, despite laws that said they must be served.

Martin graduated from Crozer at twenty-two. He was at the head of his class and gave the valedictory address. There were also other honors, among them the

Lewis Crozer Fellowship award of $1,200 in cash. This was to be applied to two more years of study at the school of his choice. Now Martin would be able to attain the highest degree in education—a doctorate.

Martin chose Boston University, and rented a room in the city. He drove back and forth to school in the green Chevrolet his parents gave him as a graduation present.

It was in Boston that Martin met the lovely Coretta Scott, who was studying voice at the New England Conservatory of Music. Like Martin, she too was from the South and had also known the whiplash of prejudice. Before their first date was over, Martin was hinting about marriage, even though they each had a year more of schooling ahead of them.

As the months passed, Martin's talk of marriage became more pressing. Coretta did not know what to do. She wanted to become a concert singer, and had hoped not to marry until her career was safely launched.

Martin, however, convinced her otherwise and they were married on June 18, 1953. The ceremony was performed by Martin's father in the garden of Coretta's home.

By the time the newlyweds had completed their last year of school, they were faced with a very serious decision. The new Dr. King had offers of teaching jobs in three colleges. Also, there were three churches, two of them in the North, that wanted Dr. King for their pastor. The third church was in the South—in Montgomery, Alabama.

Both Dr. King and his wife were tempted to turn their backs on the South where both had suffered as second-class citizens. By accepting one of the offers in the North they knew that they could lead an easier life.

Yet, the South, despite its mistreatment of Negroes, was still "home." It was

The ceremony was performed by Martin's father in the garden
of Coretta's home.

where their roots were and Martin and Coretta wanted to be back with their family and friends.

Martin accepted the pastorate of the Dexter Avenue Baptist Church in Montgomery, Alabama. Together the young couple hoped to help in shaping a brighter future for their people.

# The Spark Catches

Martin's father had objected to his decision to accept the pastorate of Dexter Avenue Baptist Church. He had hoped that Martin would stay in Atlanta as co-pastor of Ebenezer, but he had other reasons, too.

Reverend King remembered that on one visit to Montgomery many years before, he and a group of ministers had boarded a trolley. The white conductor had taken their fares at the front end, and then ordered them to get off the trolley and board it again at the Negro entrance in the back. Reverend King had refused to do this, demanding his money back. He stood his ground and a heated argument followed. Finally his friends persuaded him to get off the trolley.

Things had not changed much when his son arrived in Montgomery twenty-five years later. Buses had replaced the trolley cars, but Negroes still had to take their seats in the rear.

Dr. King was soon speaking out plainly against such injustices in his Sunday sermons. He had also started talking to other ministers and to Negro leaders in the community about Gandhi's program of civil disobedience.

"Why couldn't such a plan work in Montgomery," he wondered. "What would happen if Negroes stopped riding the buses as a protest," he asked his friends. They thought that such a plan might work *someday*.

Then one day, after Dr. King had been in Montgomery over a year, and there was still only talk among Negroes about "doing something" to help themselves, a middle-aged Negro seamstress, Mrs. Rosa Parks, *did something*. After work, she boarded a bus in downtown Montgomery, paid her fare and took the first seat behind a sign reading "Reserved for White." Three other Negroes also sat near her in the white section.

As the bus began to fill up with white passengers, the driver ordered the Negroes to stand and make room for them. The other three Negroes promptly gave up their seats. Mrs. Parks remained in hers.

Again the driver ordered her to stand. She remained in her seat. A policeman was called and Mrs. Parks was arrested and taken to jail. It was Thursday evening, December 1, 1955.

One of the first people to hear of Mrs. Parks' arrest was E. D. Nixon, a Pullman porter. He once had been state president of the NAACP (the National Association

RESERVED FOR WHITE

A policeman was called and Mrs. Parks was arrested and taken to jail.

for the Advancement of Colored People), the oldest Negro civil rights group. Mrs. Parks had been his secretary. When he was notified of her arrest, he immediately went to sign the bond for her release.

Mrs. Parks' arrest troubled Mr. Nixon deeply. He felt that it was an outrage against the Negro community. Early the next morning, Mr. Nixon called Dr. King and suggested that Negroes stop riding the buses as a protest against Mrs. Parks' arrest. Dr. King agreed that the time to boycott the buses had come.

That night, a meeting of Negro leaders was held in Dr. King's church. The ministers who were present agreed to speak to their congregations on Sunday about the tremendous importance of their refusing to ride the buses.

The group also planned to print and distribute seven thousand leaflets, notifying the Negro community of the bus boycott.

The white community soon learned of

the boycott, too. A Negro maid was given one of the leaflets, and being unable to read, asked her employer to read it to her. The white woman could hardly believe what she was reading—how *dared* they? Outraged, she called a newspaper.

By Saturday morning, the planned boycott was on page one. Dr. King and his associates were delighted—a white newspaper was giving them far better distribution than they had planned. The leaflet was reprinted word for word:

*Don't ride the bus to work, to town, to school, or anyplace Monday, December 5. If you work, take a cab, or share a ride, or walk. Come to a mass meeting, Monday at 7:00 p.m., at the Holt Street Baptist Church for further instructions.*

When Monday morning finally came, Martin and his wife were up by 5:30 to see how effective the boycott would be.

The bus line which went past their home was used by more Negroes than any other line. It was usually crowded with domestic workers in the early morning.

As they watched from a front window, they saw the first bus roll slowly by. It was empty! Fifteen minutes later, a second bus came by. It, too, was empty. The third bus carried only two *white* passengers.

Dr. King dressed hurriedly and rushed out of the house to his car. For more than an hour he cruised around, observing every bus. He counted only eight Negro passengers. On any *normal* day the buses would have been carrying some 17,500 Negroes to and from their jobs.

# Walking
# for Freedom

Mrs. Parks was fined ten dollars and court costs for disobeying the city's segregation law, which did not grant Negroes the same rights as whites. Now for the first time, there was a clear-cut test case to challenge the unjust segregation laws.

Later that afternoon, at a meeting of boycott leaders, Dr. King was unanimously elected president of a newly formed organization, *The Montgomery Improvement Association.* This group was to set policy and plan strategy for the boycott.

Returning home that evening for a few moments before the mass meeting, Dr. King told his wife that he was deeply concerned about the new responsibility that suddenly had been thrust upon him. He explained that he would no longer have much time to spend at home with her and with their two-week-old daughter, Yolanda. "And," he finished in a quiet voice, "it is only fair to warn you that there is an element of danger in all this."

Coretta listened calmly to all Martin had to say. Finally, in a reassuring voice she said, "Whatever you do, you know you have my backing. We'll worry about danger when we're in it," she added and managed a half-smile.

At the mass meeting that night, the Holt Street church was filled to overflowing and about three thousand more people were unable to get in. Loudspeakers were set up outside so that they could hear what was being said inside the church.

With unusual fervor and spiritual outpouring, the huge crowd lifted its voice in the opening hymn. With one mighty voice came the words "Onward, Christian Soldiers." Then Dr. King rose to speak and the crowd was silent. The television cameras began to roll—the bus boycott had become *News.*

"Love must be our regulating ideal," Dr. King stressed in his clear, strong voice. "Once again, we must hear the words of Jesus echoing across the centuries: 'Love your enemies, bless them that curse you, and pray for them that despitefully use you. . . .'"

"If you will protest courageously, and yet with dignity and Christian love, when the history books are written in future generations, the historians will have to pause and say, 'There lived a great people—a black people—who injected new

"Love must be our regulating ideal."

meaning and dignity into the veins of civilization.' This is our challenge and our overwhelming responsibility."

The first few days of the boycott gave it added momentum and provided the Negro community with a new sense of pride, dignity and a spirit of working together. The Negroes walked cheerfully, sometimes in the rain, and very often for great distances. Old men and women walked as well as young children. Some rode mules through the streets or drove horse-and-wagon rigs. Others rode in one of the two hundred and ten Negro-operated taxicabs, whose owners had agreed to let passengers ride at bus fare rates. New volunteer car pools were formed each day.

But they didn't ride the buses!

Soon it was obvious to the owners of the bus company and to the white community that the Negroes were not going to ride the buses unless their terms were met. They wanted only three things: courteous treatment from drivers; seating on a first-come, first-served basis, and the employment of Negro bus drivers.

The bus company and the city officials would not agree to the Negroes' terms so the boycott continued. Then city officials began a "get tough" policy with the boycotters. Car pool drivers were stopped and asked to show their licenses and insurance policies. On the smallest excuse, they were given tickets. Riders, waiting to be picked up, were threatened with arrest as "hitch-hikers." Most of the boycotters stood firm. Only a few quit the car pools, fearful that their licenses might be revoked or their insurance cancelled. Some quit because they were afraid that they could not remain nonviolent in the face of police abuse.

Then one day, Dr. King himself was arrested on a "trumped-up" charge. But he was not to be behind bars for long. News of his arrest spread quickly throughout the Negro community and everyone began heading toward the jail to see what could be done to help.

Soon, such a large crowd of well-wishers was gathered outside the jail that the jailer began to panic. He released Dr. King on his own and personally ushered him out of jail.

Before long, more violent methods were used to force the Negroes to end their boycott. Early one night, a bomb was tossed on the porch of Dr. King's home while he was at a mass meeting. Just before the bomb exploded, Coretta grabbed their infant daughter and ran to the rear of the house. Most of the front windows of the Kings' home were broken and the living room was a shambles—but Coretta and the baby were safe. Luckily Coretta had heard "something heavy drop on the front porch."

By the time Dr. King received news of the bombing and arrived at his home, an angry crowd of Negroes had gathered around his house. Police were unable to control them. Many were armed and obviously unwilling to remain nonviolent.

"If you have weapons," Dr. King said to them quietly, "take them home. If you do not have them, please do not seek to get them. We cannot solve this problem through violence. . . . Remember the words of Jesus: 'He who lives by the sword shall perish by the sword.' . . . We must meet our white brothers' hate with love."

Neither bombing, harassment nor trickery stopped the boycott, and after three months a Montgomery Grand Jury met and concluded that the boycott was illegal. They then proceeded to arrest one hundred of the boycotters and their leaders. Cheerfully, all of them surrendered and went to jail.

Dr. King received word that there was a warrant out for his arrest while he was on a speaking tour in Nashville, Tennessee. He hurried back to Montgomery and, like the others, voluntarily gave himself up.

By now the nation's press had learned of the mass arrests, and reporters and television crews swarmed into Montgomery from all over. When March 19, the time for trial arrived, the press of the world covered the event. Among them were newsmen from France and England —and from India, the liberated nation whose leader, Gandhi, had inspired Martin Luther King.

After a four-day trial, Dr. King was found guilty of "violating the state's anti-boycott law." The judge then sentenced Dr. King either to pay a fine of $500 or to serve 386 days at hard labor in the county jail. Quickly a notice of appeal was filed and Dr. King and the others were released on bond.

Two months later, on May 11, a hearing of the appeal was held in a Federal court before three judges. They took three weeks to come to a decision, but it was worth waiting for. They decided that the segregation laws governing city buses in Montgomery could not be enforced because they were unconstitutional. But total victory was not yet won.

Lawyers for the city of Montgomery now took the case to the United States Supreme Court, the highest court in the land. Once again, Montgomery lost.

On November 13, 1956, the Supreme Court also declared that Alabama's bus segregation laws were unconstitutional.

After 381 days of walking for freedom, Montgomery's 50,000 Negroes—with Martin Luther King, Jr., as their leader—had won out against injustice. They had stood together as American Negroes had never before stood together. And they had won new dignity for themselves and the respect of the world in their victory.

# We
# Shall Overcome

From this time forward, there was no turning back for Dr. King. Overnight, he found himself the leader of an awakened people. Plans were made to extend protests all over the South. A new organization was formed. It was called *SCLC* (Southern Christian Leadership Conference) and Dr. King was elected its president.

Other groups also joined the fight for freedom. White college students from the

North joined forces with Negro college students from the South. They banded together and began sit-ins at restaurants and stores which would not serve Negroes. They were met with threats and often with beatings. But they were not stopped and they did not "lose their nonviolence."

Then the *freedom rides* began. Groups of whites and Negroes from all over the country boarded buses in the South and sat together in the white section. They "tested" bus station restaurants and highway restaurants insisting that the Negroes among them had the right to be served in places of public accommodation. They were carted off to jail by the hundreds. In jail, they went on hunger strikes and sang freedom songs.

"We Shall Overcome" became the freedom-fighters' song. It was sung on picket lines at bus stations and on protest marches. People joined hands at rallies in the lonesome fields of the rural South and sang it by the light of flickering torches. As they marched to jail they sang:

> We are not afraid, we are not afraid,
> We are not afraid today
> Oh, deep in my heart I do believe
> We shall overcome some day.*

Wherever the freedom movement reached a crest, Dr. King was there to give his people courage and spiritual guidance. Older protest groups like the Urban League and the NAACP (National Association for the Advancement of Colored People) gave their support to the freedom movement. They were joined by newly formed groups like CORE (the Congress of Racial Equality) and by SNCC (the Student Non-Violent Coordinating Committee).

The clergy of all faiths joined the movement. White Episcopalian ministers were jailed for freedom riding, and Jewish rab-

* Music and further verses will be found on pages 108-09.

bis fasted and prayed in the jails of the South. A Catholic bishop insisted that the white schools in his diocese admit Negroes.

Dr. King spoke at rallies of thousands and at small gatherings in the fields. His growing family saw very little of him, but his wife, Coretta, stood firm.

Their second child, Martin Luther King III, was only a year old when a mentally ill Negro woman stabbed Dr. King with a paper knife in New York City. He was in critical condition for days.

While Mrs. King was carrying Dexter Scott, their third child, Dr. King was serving time in an Atlanta jail for leading a protest march.

A few days after Mrs. King gave birth to their youngest daughter, Bernice Albertine, Dr. King finished a week of demonstrations in Birmingham, Alabama. He led a crowd of 2,500 Negroes straight through police lines and headed downtown. They were arrested at lunch counters and on the streets. But still they came, rank on rank, dressed in their Sunday best and singing, "We Shall Overcome."

Fire hoses were turned on them and many were thrown flat by the powerful streams of water. Others took their places. All in all, 3,300 Negroes were arrested that week in Birmingham. They were carted off to jail still singing. Among them was Dr. King.

Coretta was worried. Usually when Dr. King was jailed, he was able to get word through to her. But this time he was being held in solitary confinement. Finally, in desperation she placed a call to President Kennedy to try to find out if her husband was all right, but she could not reach him. The threat of violence or of sudden death was never far from Coretta's thoughts. Early the following evening, Coretta received a long distance call. She picked up the phone and the

Fire hoses were turned on them and many were thrown
flat by the powerful streams of water.

operator said shortly, "Will you please get your child off the phone?"

Two-year-old Dexter had picked up the extension phone downstairs and was busily chattering away. He had no idea that he was interfering in affairs of state. The operator was trying to connect President Kennedy with Mrs. King! He was calling to assure her that her husband was safe and that the F.B.I. was standing by.

The Kings did not find it easy to bring up a "normal" family in the setting of Dr. King's work. The two older children, Yolanda and Dexter, began to ask why their father kept going to jail. They knew that people generally go to jail for doing wrong. Coretta assured them that their father went to jail "to help people." Still, other children teased them about it and there were hard moments.

Dr. King always tried to spend as many weekends as possible with his family and he did his best never to miss a holiday at home. But the freedom movement demanded more and more of his time. One year, he traveled 275,000 miles and made 350 speeches!

The freedom rides, the sit-ins and the protest marches kept going strong. Students tramped the red dirt roads of Georgia and swamplands of Mississippi encouraging Negroes to register and vote.

The surge toward freedom was answered by the burning of four Negro churches in Georgia. A white mailman, William Moore, walking the roads as a lone freedom marcher, was murdered in Alabama. Medgar Evers, a Negro leader, was shot to death on his own front porch in the dead of night in Mississippi—and there were other martyrs.

It was a time of trouble and terror but a time of truth and triumph, too.

# "I Have a Dream"

On August 28, 1963, a huge civil rights demonstration, *The March on Washington,* was held. It was the largest crowd ever to gather in Washington, D.C.—over a quarter of a million strong.

Young and old, Negro and white, Gentile and Jew—housewives, sharecroppers, singers, servants and statesmen—gathered on the slope of the Washington Monument. Shoulder to shoulder, they marched to the Lincoln Memorial.

They had poured into Washington by the busload. They had jammed the wait-

Shoulder to shoulder, they marched to the Lincoln Memorial.

ing rooms of hundreds of small railway stations. Seats on planes were not to be found and car pools inched forward, bumper to bumper, on the roads that led into Washington—from the North, South, East and West.

Many came from overseas, too—diplomats from the new African nations and press representatives from the capitals of Europe.

Weeks before the great day, an eighty-two-year-old man left Dayton, Ohio, for the March on a silver bicycle. A civil rights worker made the trip from Chicago to Washington on roller skates.

The Military Police were out in full force, too. Businessmen and officials feared that violence might break out in such a huge crowd. But there was no violence. The crowd had learned the lessons of Martin Luther King too well.

He stood before them, dwarfed by the brooding statue of Abraham Lincoln, and he said: "I have a dream that one day on the red hills of Georgia the sons of former slaves and the sons of former slaveowners will be able to sit down together at the table of brotherhood. . . . We will be able to speed up that day when all of God's children . . . join in the words of the old Negro spiritual, 'Free at last! free at last! Thank God Almighty, we are free at last!' "*

The March on Washington gave the civil rights movement new importance. Dr. King and other Negro leaders were asked to help draft a bill that would give the Negro equal rights. *Time* magazine chose Dr. King as "The Man of the Year," and used his picture on its cover. He was given several honorary degrees, including a Doctor of Laws from Yale University.

Officials who had seen the tremendous show of strength that the March expressed began to take an interest in the

---

* Complete text of this speech will be found on pages 110-18.

*Civil Rights Bill* that President Kennedy had proposed.

But the days of wrath were not yet over. On Sunday morning, September 15th, a Negro church, which had been used for civil rights meetings, was bombed. Four little girls were killed as they recited their Sunday school lessons. Later that day, two teen-age Negro boys were shot and killed from ambush.

People of good will everywhere were deeply shocked by the murders of these innocent children. Demands for a strong Civil Rights Bill came from all sides. It was feared that the Negroes' self-control might snap if such a bill was not soon made law.

Before he was assassinated on November 22, 1963, President Kennedy presented a Civil Rights Bill to Congress. The bill was passed by the House of Representatives but was held up by the Senate for many months. It was finally passed by the members of the Senate and signed by President Johnson on July 2, 1964.

With the passage of the Civil Rights Bill, the American Negro at last had his foot on the road toward freedom.

Martin Luther King, Jr., stated his people's new position when he finished a speech by saying: "I say good night to you by quoting an old Negro slave preacher who said, 'We ain't what we ought to be, and we ain't what we want to be, and we ain't what we're going to be. But thank God, we ain't what we was.'"

# The Prize Is Won

On October 14, 1964, Martin Luther King, Jr., took his place among the great men of all lands who have fought for the cause of peace. On that day, it was announced that the young Negro leader had won the Nobel Peace Prize.

The prize, which was first awarded in 1901, was named in honor of its donor, Alfred Bernhard Nobel, the Swedish chemist who invented dynamite. The Peace Prize is one of five Nobel prizes which are given each year that worthy recipients can be found. It is awarded "without distinction of nationality."

Besides the Peace Prize, there are three Nobel prizes given—for eminence in the fields of chemistry, medicine and physics. A fourth prize is awarded to the author of a literary work of true idealism.

At thirty-five, Dr. King was the youngest person ever to win the award, and the second American Negro. The first was Dr. Ralph J. Bunche who won the Peace Prize for his work as a United Nations Under-Secretary.

The prize carries a cash award of $54,000 which Dr. King donated to the civil rights movement. The Nobel medal and diploma were presented to Dr. King in Oslo, Norway, on December 10, 1964, by Gunnar Jahn, the chairman of the Nobel Peace Prize Committee. The ceremony took place on the anniversary of Dr. Nobel's death in 1896.

Dr. King arrived in Oslo on a special chartered flight. With him were his wife, his father and mother, his brother and sisters and many of the civil rights leaders who had fought side by side with him for so long. Their memories of the long years of struggle were plain to see as they stood in the great hall of Oslo University. With pride, they watched a distinguished audience of world dignitaries, including King Olaf V of Norway, rise in a standing ovation for the simple Baptist minister from Atlanta.

In his presentation speech, Dr. Jahn described Dr. King as "an undaunted champion of peace . . . the first person in the Western World to have shown us that a struggle can be waged without violence." He spoke of Dr. King as one who has "suffered for his faith, been imprisoned on many occasions, whose home has been subject to bomb attacks, whose life and those of his family have been threatened, and who nevertheless has never faltered."

Dr. King's rich, compelling voice easily

filled the huge hall as he acknowledged the award, saying: "I accept the Nobel prize for peace at a moment when twenty-two million Negroes of the United States of America are engaged in a creative battle to end the long night of racial injustice. I accept this award in behalf of a civil rights movement which is moving with determination and a majestic scorn for risk and danger to establish a reign of freedom and a rule of justice.

"I come as a trustee, for in the depths of my heart I am aware that this prize is much more than an honor to me personally. . . . You honor the ground crew without whose labor and sacrifices the jet flights to freedom could never have left the earth.

"Most of these people will never make the headlines and their names will not appear in Who's Who. Yet when the years have rolled past and the blazing light of truth is focused on this marvelous age in which we live—men and women will

The Nobel medal and diploma being presented to
Dr. King by Dr. Gunnar Jahn.

know, and children will be taught, that we have a finer land, a better people, a more noble civilization—because these humble children of God were willing to suffer for righteousness' sake."

# "Free at Last"

When Dr. Martin Luther King, Jr., arrived in Memphis, Tennessee, on April 3, 1968, he was welcomed by a crowd of over two thousand supporters. Dr. King had been invited to Memphis to lead a march on behalf of the city's garbage workers who were striking for higher wages. The strike had become a civil rights cause, since more than ninety percent of the workers were Negroes.

On an earlier trip to Memphis, Dr. King had led a march on behalf of the strikers that ended in violence. One person was killed and many were injured and there were over two hundred arrests. The violence, created by some young Black Nationalist activists, depressed Dr. King for it was the first time in his civil rights career that violence had erupted. This kind of outbreak suddenly threatened his whole philosophy of nonviolence. He was faced with a terrible decision. Should he return to Memphis and try to conduct another non-violent march or yield to the possibility of further violence? This period of indecision plagued Dr. King for several days. His first thought was to get out of Memphis and never return, but then he said, "This is no time to quit. Nothing could be more tragic than to stop at this point."

He went back to Atlanta, gathered his SCLC staff together and made plans of strategy to lead a peaceful non-violent march through the streets of Memphis to support the garbage workers' strike. And so it was that on Wednesday, April 3, he

returned to Memphis to face the supreme
test of his theory of non-violence.

All day on Thursday, April 4, Dr. King
met with his staff in Room 306 of the
Negro-owned and operated Lorraine Motel in Memphis. At the end of this trying
day, Dr. King dressed for dinner and
stepped out on the balcony of his motel
at about 6 P.M. to join his staff, many of
whom had already begun to leave for the
home of the Reverend Kyles, their dinner
host. Dr. King had looked forward to the
dinner, anticipating the period of relax-
ation before going to the evening mass
meeting.

Dressed in his usual public attire—
black suit, tie and white shirt—Dr. King
leaned over the iron rail of the balcony
and chatted with his staff aides who were
standing below in the courtyard of the
motel waiting for him.

Suddenly a shot rang out. Some said it
sounded like a stick of dynamite . . .
another witness reported it sounded like a

Dr. King leaned over the iron rail of the balcony and chatted with his staff aides—About that time a shot rang out . . .

firecracker . . . another thought it was an automobile accident and still others said it had the sound of a bomb. The sharp sound was unusual and unexpected.

The Reverend Ralph Abernathy, Dr. King's long-time friend and close associate, rushed out of Room 306 to investigate the noise and saw the fallen King stretched out on the concrete floor. Abernathy knelt down beside him and tried to speak to him but the famed, prophetic speaker was now speechless.

An ambulance was summoned by the police and arrived about fifteen minutes later. At 7:05 P.M. at St. Joseph's Hospital, an assistant hospital administrator called together King's tense and nervous staff and read a brief but concise statement. It said, "At 7 P.M. Dr. Martin Luther King expired in the emergency room of a gunshot wound in the neck."

Thursday, April 4, became a black date soon to be recorded in history as the day the voice of non-violence was silenced by an act of violence. Dr. King, the famous American citizen who won the 1964 Nobel Prize for consistently asserting the principle of non-violence, was gunned down by an assassin who, with a single bullet, asserted his principle of violence.

The Peaceful Warrior was gone and with him peace and tranquility in our cities. Violence erupted in the nation's capital, and almost simultaneously, civil disorders broke out in forty-six cities. The senseless murder of this famed American ignited an emotional bonfire across the country. Angry Negroes spilled into the streets of numerous cities reacting against the assassination of Dr. King, their fallen leader. Stores were burned, cars overturned, windows smashed, rocks thrown and people were killed and injured. Within a week, the riots brought on by the death of Dr. King had claimed thirty-nine lives. The assassination had provoked the kinds of emotions that produced an antithesis to his life—violence and death.

The President of the United States, Lyndon B. Johnson, spoke to Americans on radio and television and said, "We have been saddened by the assassination of Dr. King. I ask every citizen to reject the blind violence that has struck Dr. King who lived by non-violence." He later issued a proclamation:

I, Lyndon B. Johnson, President of the United States, do call upon all Americans to observe next Sunday, the 7th of April, as the day of national mourning throughout the United States. . . . I direct that until interment, the flag of the United States shall be flown at half-staff on all buildings, grounds and naval vessels of the federal government in the District of Columbia and throughout the United States and its territories and possessions.

Dr. King's body went on public view Saturday afternoon, April 6, in the Chapel of Spelman College (a part of the Atlanta University system where Dr. King had gone to college) and remained there until Monday afternoon when it was removed and carried to Ebenezer Baptist Church, co-pastored by the father-son team of Dr. Martin Luther King, Sr. and Jr. There it remained until the funeral services which were held Tuesday morning, April 9.

More than 50,000 mourners passed by— some quietly, others sobbing. Some cried aloud and others were near collapse. Many children passed by Dr. King's body. Some were so little that they had to be lifted by their parents to see the body in the glass-covered coffin.

In the wake of Dr. King's death, the overwhelming public response was one of grief and regret. Tributes came in from everywhere. They came from black and white, rich and poor, from home and abroad, from the young and the old. His children received numerous letters of sympathy and many invitations to spend their vacations with other children. One little boy wrote, "I feel so sorry that you lost your daddy. I'll be glad to share mine with you."

While preparations for the final rites were being completed in Atlanta, dignitaries and plain people were streaming into the city by the thousands. People came from everywhere—ministers from St. Louis, brick masons from Detroit, garbage workers from Memphis, Congressmen from Washington, movie stars from Hollywood, friends from foreign lands, and thousands of others.

The public service was held on the campus of Morehouse College where Martin Luther King received his undergraduate degree and was regarded as the most outstanding alumnus of the institution.

There were so many people on the campus and the crowd was so crushing that the services had to be shortened. A number of people became ill and several fainted. After the services, the ride to the graveside began.

The Reverend Ralph Abernathy officiated at the final service and said, "The cemetery is too small for his spirit but we commit his body to the ground."

Mrs. King sat still and strong as she listened and watched. The children had tears in their eyes. They joined their mother in putting their hands on the coffin before it was rolled into the Georgia marble crypt. Some very simple words form the epitaph on the crypt. They are words from an old slave song that Dr. King often used to end his speeches. They probably would be his words now if he could speak them—"Free at last, free at last, thank God Almighty, I'm free at last."

"Free at last, free at last, thank God Almighty I'm free at last!"

# A SHORT BIBLIOGRAPHY OF BOOKS ON NEGROES AND THE CIVIL RIGHTS MOVEMENT

(starting with the easiest ones)

THE FIRST BOOK OF NEGROES
by Langston Hughes (Franklin Watts)
GREAT AMERICAN NEGROES
revised by Ben Richardson (Crowell)
CARVER'S GEORGE
by Florence Crannell Means
(Houghton Mifflin)
FREDERICK DOUGLASS: *Slave, Fighter,
Freeman* by Arna Bontemps (Knopf)
MARY MCLEOD BETHUNE
by Emma Gelders Sterne (Knopf)
FREEDOM TRAIN: *The Story of
Harriet Tubman* by Dorothy Sterling
(Doubleday)

## Bibliography

THE STORY OF PHILLIS WHEATLEY
  by Shirley Graham (Messner)
THE PEACEABLE REVOLUTION
  by Betty Schechter (Houghton Mifflin)
MARTIN LUTHER KING
  by Doris and Harold Faber (Messner)
HARRIET TUBMAN: *Conductor on the
  Underground Railroad* by Ann Petry
  (Archway Paperbacks published by Pocket
  Books)

### ADULT TITLES

THE AMERICAN NEGRO REFERENCE BOOK
  edited by John P. Davis (Prentice-Hall)
A PICTORIAL HISTORY OF THE NEGRO
  IN AMERICA
  by Langston Hughes and Milton Meltzer
  (Crown)
THE SOULS OF BLACK FOLK
  by William E. B. Du Bois (Peter Smith)
UP FROM SLAVERY
  by Booker T. Washington (Doubleday)
IN THEIR OWN WORDS
  by Milton Meltzer (Crowell)
THE SCLC STORY IN WORDS AND PICTURES
  edited by Ed Clayton
  (An SCLS Publication—paper)

# "We Shall Overcome"

New Words and Music Arrangement by
Zilphia Horton, Frank Hamilton,
Guy Carawan and Pete Seeger

Arr. Charity Bailey

2. We are not afraid, we are not afraid,
   We are not afraid today,
   Oh, deep in my heart I do believe
   We shall overcome some day.

3. We'll walk hand in hand, we'll walk hand in hand,
   We'll walk hand in hand some day,
   Oh, deep in my heart I do believe
   We shall overcome some day.

4. The truth will make us free, the truth will make us free,
   The truth will make us free some day,
   Oh, deep in my heart I do believe
   We shall overcome some day.

5. We shall live in peace, we shall live in peace,
   We shall live in peace some day,
   Oh, deep in my heart I do believe
   We shall overcome some day.

### About "We Shall Overcome"

The song as we know it today was composed by Mrs. Zilphia Horton at the Highlander Folk School in Tennessee, with new verses and other matter added by Guy Carawan, Frank Hamilton and Pete Seeger.

Mrs. Horton's version may have been inspired by a gospel hymn called "I'll Overcome Some Day" by C. Albert Tindley, which was published in 1901.

Since "We Shall Overcome" has become the Freedom Movement song, it is almost always sung at the close of civil rights meetings. People often add new verses if there is something special to sing about.

This piano arrangement by Charity Bailey includes chords for guitar or autoharp.

\* Royalties derived from this composition are being contributed to the Freedom Movement under the trusteeship of the writers.

The following is Dr. Martin Luther King's "I Have a Dream" speech, which was made at the Lincoln Memorial in Washington, D.C., on the occasion of the Civil Rights March on Washington on August 28, 1963.

# I Have a Dream

by MARTIN LUTHER KING, JR.

Five score* years ago, a great American, in whose symbolic shadow we stand, signed the Emancipation Proclamation. This momentous decree came as a great beacon light of hope to millions of Negro slaves who had been seared in

---

*five score*—one hundred years ago, during the Civil War, Lincoln signed the Emancipation Proclamation freeing the slaves in the states that had left the Union. The Thirteenth Amendment officially ended slavery in the United States.

the flames of withering injustice. It came as a joyous daybreak to end the long night of captivity.

But one hundred years later, we must face the tragic fact that the Negro is still not free. One hundred years later, the life of the Negro is still sadly crippled by the manacles of segregation and the chains of discrimination. One hundred years later, the Negro lives on a lonely island of poverty in the midst of a vast ocean of material prosperity. One hundred years later, the Negro is still languishing in the corners of American society and finds himself an exile in his own land. So we have come here today to dramatize an appalling condition.

In a sense we have come to our nation's capital to cash a check. When the architects of our republic wrote the magnificent words of the Constitution and the Declaration of Independence, they were signing a promissory note to which every American was to fall heir. This note was a promise that all men would be guaranteed the inalienable rights of life, liberty, and the pursuit of happiness.

It is obvious today that America has defaulted on this promissory note insofar as her citizens of color are concerned. Instead of honoring this sacred obligation, America has given the Negro people a bad check; a check which has come back marked "insufficient funds." But we refuse to believe that the bank of justice is bankrupt. We refuse to believe that there are insufficient funds in the great vaults of opportunity of this nation. So we have come to cash this check —a check that will give us upon demand the riches of freedom and the security of justice. We have also come to this hallowed spot to remind America of the fierce urgency of now. This is no time to engage in the luxury of cooling off or to take the tranquilizing drug of gradualism. *Now* is the time to rise from the dark and desolate valley of segregation to the sunlit path of racial justice. *Now* is the time to open the doors of opportunity to all of God's children. Now is the time to lift our nation from the quicksands of racial injustice to the solid rock of brotherhood.

It would be fatal for the nation to overlook the urgency of the moment and to underestimate the determination of the Negro. This sweltering summer of the Negro's legitimate discontent will not pass until there is an invigorating autumn of freedom and equality. Nineteen sixty-three is not an end, but a beginning. Those who hope that the

Negro needed to blow off steam and will now be content will have a rude awakening if the nation returns to business as usual. There will be neither rest nor tranquility in America until the Negro is granted his citizenship rights. The whirlwinds of revolt will continue to shake the foundations of our nation until the bright day of justice emerges.

But there is something that I must say to my people who stand on the warm threshold which leads into the palace of justice. In the process of gaining our rightful place we must not be guilty of wrongful deeds. Let us not seek to satisfy our thirst for freedom by drinking from the cup of bitterness and hatred.

We must forever conduct our struggle on the high plane of dignity and discipline. We must not allow our creative protest to degenerate into physical violence. Again and again we must rise to the majestic heights of meeting physical force with soul force. The marvelous new militancy which has engulfed the Negro community must not lead us to distrust of all white people, for many of our white brothers, as evidenced by their presence here today, have come to realize that their destiny is tied up with our destiny and their freedom is inextricably bound to our freedom. We cannot walk alone.

And as we walk, we must make the pledge that we shall march ahead. We cannot turn back. There are those who are asking the devotees of civil rights, "When will you be satisfied?" We can never be satisfied as long as the Negro is the victim of unspeakable horrors of police brutality. We can never be satisfied as long as our bodies, heavy with the fatigue of travel, cannot gain lodging in the motels of the highways and the hotels of the cities. We cannot be satisfied as long as the Negro's basic mobility is from a smaller ghetto to a larger one. We can never be satisfied as long as a Negro in Mississippi cannot vote and a Negro in New York believes he has nothing for which to vote. No, no, we are not satisfied, and we will not be satisfied until justice rolls down like waters and righteousness like a mighty stream.

I am not unmindful that some of you have come here out of great trials and tribulations. Some of you have come fresh from narrow cells. Some of you have come from areas where your quest for freedom left you battered by the storms of persecution and staggered by the winds of police brutality. You have been the veterans of creative suffering. Continue to work with the faith that unearned suffering is redemptive.

Go back to Mississippi, go back to Alabama, go back to Georgia, go back to Louisiana, go back to the slums and ghettos of our northern cities, knowing that somehow this situation can and will be changed. Let us not wallow in the valley of despair.

I say to you today, my friends, that in spite of the difficulties and frustrations of the moment, I still have a dream. It is a dream deeply rooted in the American dream.

I have a dream that one day this nation will rise up and live out the true meaning of its creed: "We hold these truths to be self-evident: that all men are created equal."

I have a dream that one day on the red hills of Georgia the sons of former slaves and the sons of former slaveowners will be able to sit down together at the table of brotherhood.

I have a dream that one day even the state of Mississippi, a desert state, sweltering with the heat of injustice and oppression, will be transformed into an oasis of freedom and justice.

I have a dream that my four little children will one day live in a nation where they will not be judged by the color of their skin but by the content of their character.

I have a dream today.

I have a dream that one day the state of Alabama, whose governor's lips are presently dripping with the words of interposition and nullification, will be transformed into a situation where little black boys and black girls will be able to join hands with little white boys and white girls and walk together as sisters and brothers.

I have a dream today.

I have a dream that one day every valley shall be exalted, every hill and mountain shall be made low, the rough places will be made plain, and the crooked places will be made straight, and the glory of the Lord shall be revealed, and all flesh shall see it together.

This is our hope. This is the faith with which I return to the South. With this faith we will be able to hew out of the mountain of despair a stone of hope. With this faith we will be able to transform the jangling discords of our nation into a beautiful symphony of brotherhood. With this faith we will be able to work together, to pray together, to struggle together, to go to jail together, to stand up for freedom together, knowing that we will be free one day.

This will be the day when all of God's children will be able to sing with a new meaning, "My country, 'tis of thee, sweet land of liberty, of thee I sing. Land where my fathers died, land of the pilgrim's pride, from every mountainside, let freedom ring."

And if America is to be a great nation this must become true. So let freedom ring from the prodigious hilltops of New Hampshire. Let freedom ring from the mighty mountains of New York. Let freedom ring from the heightening Alleghenies of Pennsylvania!

Let freedom ring from the snowcapped Rockies of Colorado!

Let freedom ring from the curvaceous peaks of California!

But not only that; let freedom ring from Stone Mountain of Georgia!

Let freedom ring from Lookout Mountain of Tennessee!

Let freedom ring from every hill and molehill of Mississippi. From every mountainside, let freedom ring.

When we let freedom ring, when we let it ring

from every village and every hamlet, from every state and every city, we will be able to speed up that day when all of God's children, black men and white men, Jews and Gentiles, Protestants and Catholics, will be able to join hands and sing in the words of the old Negro spiritual, "Free at last! free at last! thank God Almighty, we are free at last!"

## AFTERWORD

In 1983, the Congress of the United States set up a federal holiday commemorating the life of Martin Luther King, Jr. Each year, the third Monday in January will be set aside to honor Dr. King and to remember how his leadership helped to change the lives of millions of Americans. The only other American with a federal holiday in his honor is George Washington.

At the ceremony for the signing of the bill establishing the holiday, President Ronald Reagan said that Dr. King's life "symbolized what was right about America, what was noblest and best." Mrs. King urged that when remembering Dr. King we should all "make ourselves worthy to carry on his dream."

## ABOUT THE AUTHOR
## AND ILLUSTRATOR

ED CLAYTON was a well-known editor, author, and reporter. Born in Louisville, Kentucky, he went to Kentucky State College where he was class president and edited the school paper. Mr. Clayton worked on special writing assignments for *Life*, and contributed feature articles to The Associated Press, United Press International, and The Associated Negro Press. He also served as an editor with *Jet, Ebony,* and the *Negro Digest*. Ed Clayton, until his death in 1966, was an associate of Dr. King's at the Southern Christian Leadership Conference.

DAVID HODGES is a free-lance commercial artist and has worked for leading advertising agencies and book publishers. Born in Brooklyn, he attended the Leonardo da Vinci School of Fine Arts and the Art Students League. Mr. Hodges, who is married and has a grown daughter, Donna Marie, lives in St. Albans, New York.